Vaughan Williams for Choirs 1

JOHN LEAVITT

10 sacred pieces compiled and arranged for
accompanied mixed voices

MUSIC DEPARTMENT

OXFORD

UNIVERSITY PRESS

OXFORD
UNIVERSITY PRESS

Great Clarendon Street, Oxford OX2 6DP,
United Kingdom

Oxford University Press is a department of the University of Oxford.
It furthers the University's objective of excellence in research, scholarship,
and education by publishing worldwide. Oxford is a registered trade mark of
Oxford University Press in the UK and in certain other countries

First published 2020

Impression: 1

ISBN 978-0-19-353210-6

Music origination by Andrew Jones
Text origination by Michael Durnin
Printed in Great Britain on acid-free paper by
Halstan & Co. Ltd, Amersham, Bucks.

Contents

Preface

Welcome to this collection of new arrangements of short choral pieces by one of the finest British composers of the twentieth century. Born in 1872 in Gloucestershire, Ralph Vaughan Williams attended the Royal College of Music and read history and music at Trinity College, Cambridge. He studied composition with C. Hubert H. Parry and Charles Villiers Stanford, and received further tuition overseas from Max Bruch and Maurice Ravel. After a distinguished career, producing a particularly wide-ranging catalogue of works, Vaughan Williams died on 26 August 1958. His ashes were interred at Westminster Abbey.

Vaughan Williams's various musical activities—from choir master, editor, and folk-song collector to composer and conductor—greatly enhanced British musical life; but they also contributed to a mistaken view that his original composition was in some way parochial, designed for domestic consumption. He believed in the value of music education, and wrote pieces for amateurs and service music for the church; but he also displayed great sensitivity to the twentieth-century human condition, projecting a message of peace and reconciliation in works such as *Dona Nobis Pacem* (1936). Moreover, he wrote works of great artistic integrity and imagination that have stood the test of time, not least for choirs, and for all levels of music making.

Vaughan Williams was inspired by great literature and by a lifelong belief that the voice 'can be made the medium of the best and deepest human emotion' (*Vaughan Williams on Music*, ed. D. Manning, Oxford, 2007). Made up of two volumes and organized into sacred and secular works, the current collection is designed to introduce new generations of choral conductors and choirs to Vaughan Williams, sharing his music's variety and timeless quality. There is a mix of familiar and unfamiliar titles. A second aim was to make the pieces, where necessary, match today's scoring and performance needs, improving accessibility and extending their usefulness in a way that would have appealed to Vaughan Williams. At one extreme the arrangements have new piano parts for unaccompanied sections, for example, to lend support, or contain small judicious cuts. Others are arranged in a friendlier key (taking into account the range, also), or for SATB choir from a unison or treble-voice original—the subject matter and content lending itself equally well to adults. At the other end, pieces were selected for their ongoing appeal and suitability, requiring no more than light editorial amendments. In all cases, the harmony, words, and dynamics are unaltered, and my aim has been to respect the integrity and spirit of the original work.

The following commentary, on individual pieces, specifies the changes, sources, and possible uses in performance.

Finally, I wish to record my thanks to Oxford University Press for assisting my research and allowing access to its extensive catalogue, and to The Vaughan Williams Charitable Trust for its kind support.

John Leavitt
2019

Notes on the pieces

The blessed son of God from the cantata 'Hodie'

Source: 'Two Chorals', OUP, 1954
Suggested programming: Christmas (concert or church)

A piano accompaniment has been added which conforms to the original harmonic structure of the choral parts. A short introduction has been added, and the first verse is now scored for tutti sopranos or an optional solo. The piano pedalling should be modest and appropriate to the harmonic changes.

No sad thought his soul affright from the cantata 'Hodie'

Source: 'Two Chorals', OUP, 1954
Suggested programming: Christmas (concert or church)

This piece has been lowered by a semitone to C major, making it easier to read, and with a more accessible tenor part. A piano accompaniment has been added which conforms to the original harmonic structure of the choral parts. It was common for composers of music from this period to extend the dynamic range. In this case the markings *pp* and *ppp* may need to be adjusted, depending on the size and capability of the ensemble, to achieve a hushed, intimate sound. The piano pedalling should be modest and appropriate to the harmonic changes.

A Song of Thanksgiving

Source: 'A Song of Thanksgiving', OUP, 1945
Suggested programming: Concert or church (Thanksgiving, general praise)

This large work has been edited down to the first 125 bars/measures to make it a suitable length for a general anthem of thanksgiving. There is an optional shortened ending after bar/measure 116. The piano pedalling should be modest and appropriate to the harmonic changes.

This is the truth

Source: 'This is the truth', OUP, 1954
Suggested programming: Christmas (concert or church)

This unison arrangement has been reworked into a setting for SATB chorus with an optional soloist. The harmony of the SATB parts conforms to the original harmony of the piano part. Some mild figuration has also been added occasionally to the piano part in the first section of the piece. The piano pedalling should be used sparingly so as not to blur the musical lines.

O taste and see, a setting of Psalm 34: 8

Source: 'O Taste and See', OUP, 1953
Suggested programming: Church (Wedding, All Saints, 23rd Sunday after Pentecost)

This piece was written and first performed for the coronation of Queen Elizabeth II. The only change applies to the *colla parte* piano part from bar/measure 13 to the end, where it is indicated that the piano may optionally double the voices, either for support or colour. If the piano is used, it should be played *secco*.

God rest you merry, gentlemen

Source: 'God Rest You Merry', for SA chorus and piano, OUP, 1954, renewed in the USA, 1982
Suggested programming: Christmas (concert or church)

This piece was originally arranged by Vaughan Williams for SA voices and piano. Here, it has been rearranged for SATB voices and piano. The new vocal parts conform to the original harmonic structure. The piano pedalling for this arrangement should be used sparingly so as not to blur the musical lines.

O how amiable

Source: 'O how amiable', OUP, 1940
Suggested programming: Church dedication, or other festivals

Some slight adjustments have been made to the organ part to adapt it for the piano, including octave displacements, added octaves, and deleted octaves. Vaughan Williams marked much of the original organ part with slurs, which suggests a *legato* feel. If the piano pedal is used at all, then it should be used sparingly and for colour.

He that is down need fear no fall

Source: 'He that is down need fear no fall', Oxford Choral Songs (unison and piano), OUP, 1950
Suggested programming: Concert or funeral

This unison anthem has been reworked into a setting for SATB choir with an optional soloist. The harmony of the SATB parts conforms to the original harmony of the piano part. If the piano pedal is used at all, then it should be used sparingly, without blurring the musical lines.

At the name of Jesus

Source: 'At the name of Jesus', OUP, 1927, renewed in the USA, 1955
Suggested programming: Church (Ascension, Feast of Christ the King, Fourth Sunday in Advent)

Some small changes have been made in the dispensation of the forces in the choral parts. In the original, all voices sing verses 1 and 2 in unison; in this arrangement the upper voices sing verse 1 and the lower voices sing verse 2. In verses 4 and 6 some sopranos sing the descant and the remaining SATB choir sing in unison. A light optional piano accompaniment has been added in verse 5. Verse 7 has been arranged for SATB instead of unison voices. In the final phrase the sopranos sing a short descant for a stronger ending, with the tenors and sopranos singing in a higher tessitura. The harmony of any changes to the choral parts conforms to the original harmonic structure. The piano pedal should be used sparingly and avoid blurring the musical lines. It should not be used at all in the section with the staccato left-hand bass (verse 5).

Let us now praise famous men

Source: 'The New Church Anthem Book', OUP, 1992
Suggested programming: Church (All Saints)

This unison anthem has been revoiced for SATB choir. The harmony of the SATB parts conforms to the original harmony of the piano part. The pedal should not be used for most of this piece.

The blessed son of God

from the cantata 'Hodie'

Miles Coverdale (1487–1569),
after Martin Luther

RALPH VAUGHAN WILLIAMS (1872–1958)
piano arranged by John Leavitt

Duration: *c*.2 mins

our poor flesh and our poor__ blood Was clothed that ev - er -

-last - ing good. Ky - ri - e - lei - son.__

*Lord__ have mer - cy.*__

TUTTI
***p** dolce*

S.

The Lord Christ Je - su, God's son__ dear, Was a guest and a

***p** dolce*

A.

The Lord Christ__ Je - su, God's son__ dear, Was a guest and a

***p** dolce*

T.

The Lord Christ Je - su, God's son__ dear, Was a guest and a

***p** dolce*

B.

The Lord Christ__ Je - su, God's son__ dear, Was a guest and a

***p** dolce*

No sad thought his soul affright

from the cantata 'Hodie'

Verse 1: Anon.
Verse 2: Ursula Vaughan Williams (1911–2007)

RALPH VAUGHAN WILLIAMS (1872–1958)
piano arranged by John Leavitt

Duration: c.2.5 mins

This piece has been lowered a semitone from the original.

© Oxford University Press 1954 and 2020. Words reprinted by kind permission.

A Song of Thanksgiving

Song of the Three Holy Children, v. 29–31, 33
Henry V, Act IV, Scene 8
1 Chronicles 29: 11
Song of the Three Holy Children, v. 67

RALPH VAUGHAN WILLIAMS (1872–1958)
edited by John Leavitt

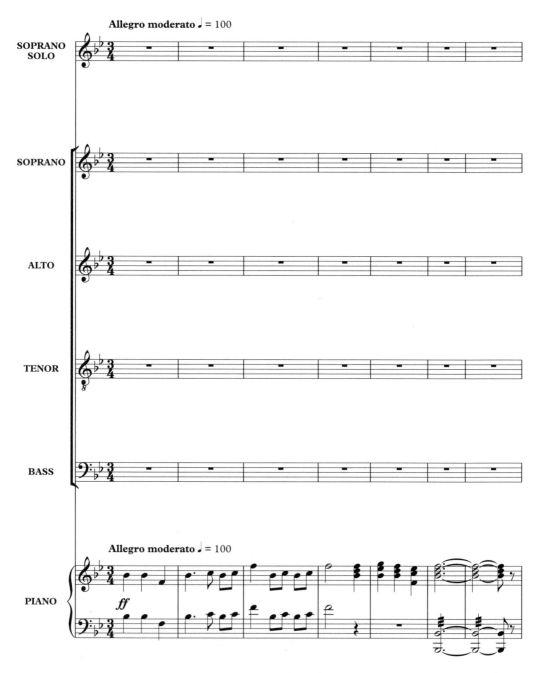

Duration: *c.*3.5 mins

SOPRANO SOLO (or SOLI)

Bless-ed art thou, O Lord God of our fa - thers; _____ and to be praised and ex-alt - ed a - bove all for ev - -er. _____

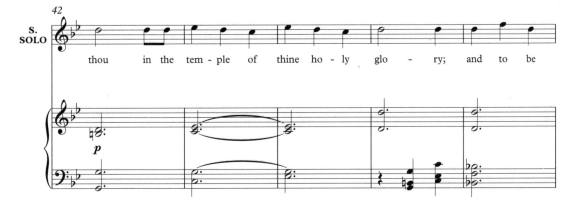

thou   in the tem - ple of thine ho - ly glo - ry; and to be

praised and ex - alt - ed a - bove all for ev - er.

Bless - ed art thou on the glo -

Bless - ed art thou on the glo -

Bless - ed art thou on the glo -

Bless - ed art thou on the glo -

Speaker: the notation is purely conventional and does not imply any particular pitch, and need not be in absolute strict time, but must finish at the places where the piano and chorus swell up, through measure/bar 74.

not to us, but to thy arm a - lone a-scribe we all.

ev - er,_____ for__ ev - - -

ev - er, for__ ev - er, for__ ev - -

ev - - er, for ev -

ev - er, for

pp

* This is only a 'safety' pause. If the speaker has already reached the last word then go on at once to the next bar.

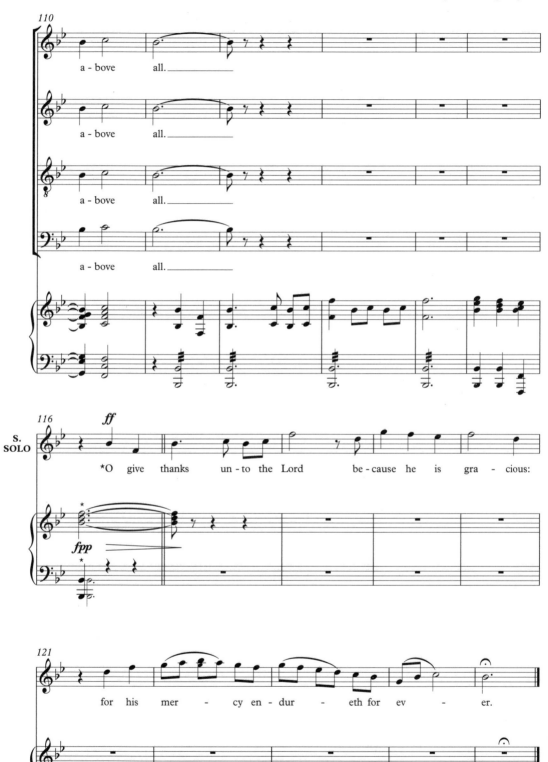

* Optional ending: for this final chord the left hand holds the same value as the right hand (see cue-sized note) and ends at the double bar, omitting the final vocal solo.

This is the truth

Trad. English

arr. by RALPH VAUGHAN WILLIAMS (1872–1958)
arr. for SATB choir and piano by John Leavitt

Duration: c.2 mins

* Sopranos sing in the absence of a soloist: either tutti or soli.

from your door, But hearken all both rich and poor.

oo

2. The

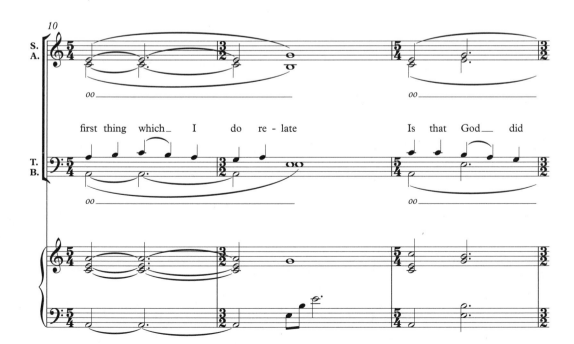

first thing which I do re - late Is that God did

inter-pose;_____ And so a pro - mise_____ soon did run_____ That

he would re - deem us by__ his Son.__ 4. And__ at that sea - son

of the year_____ Our blest Re - deem - er did ap - pear;_____ He__

here did live,___ and___ here did preach, And ma - ny___ thou - sands___

DESCANT (OPT.)

5. Thus___ he_____ to

S.
A.

he__ did teach._____ 5. Thus he in love___ to

T.
B.

us be - haved,____ To show us_____

us be- haved, To show us how we____ must be saved; And__

T.

B.

__ how we must be saved;_____ Be__ pleased to hear____

if you want to____ know the way, Be__ pleased to hear__ what he

what he did say, to hear

did say, to hear

S. SOLO what he did say.

S. A. what he did say.

T. B.

O taste and see

Psalm 34: 8

RALPH VAUGHAN WILLIAMS (1872–1958)
edited by John Leavitt

Duration: *c*.1 min

This motet may be sung in the key of G flat.

* Optional: the voice parts may be doubled by the piano, if desired.

* Optional doubling of voices.

God rest you merry, gentlemen

Trad. English

arr. RALPH VAUGHAN WILLIAMS (1872–1958)
arr. for SATB choir by John Leavitt

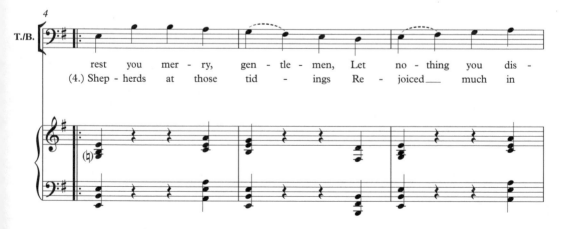

Duration: *c*.3 mins

-may, Re - mem - ber Christ our Sa - viour was
mind, And left their flocks a - feed - ing In

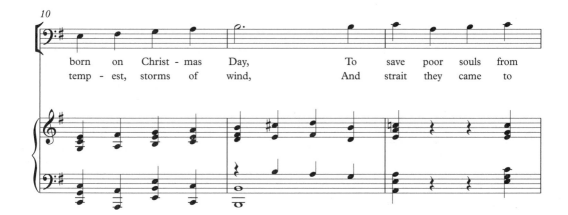

born on Christ - mas Day, To save poor souls from
temp - est, storms of wind, And strait they came to

S./A.

unis. *f*

And it's

T./B.

Sa - tan's pow'r Which had long time gone a - stray,
Beth - le - hem, The Son of God to find.

f

f

tid - ings of com - fort and joy, com-fort and

joy: And it's tid - ings of com - fort and joy.

S. *p*

A.
2. In
5. Now

p

p

Beth - le - hem in Jew - ry this bless - ed babe was
when they came to Beth - le - hem, Where our sweet Sa - viour

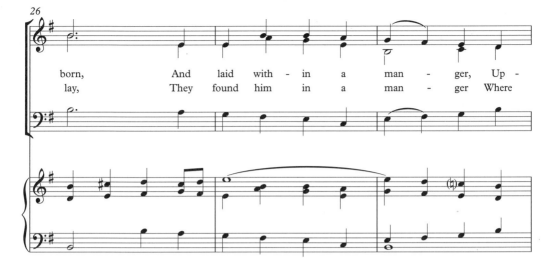

born,   And   laid   with - in   a   man   -   ger,   Up -
lay,   They found him   in   a   man   -   ger   Where

-on   this bless - ed_ morn;   The   which his   mo - ther
ox - en feed on_ hay,   The   bless - ed   Vir - gin

T.

B.

unis.

Ma - ry No - thing did take in scorn: And it's
kneel - ing_ down, Un - to the Lord did pray.

unis.

marcato

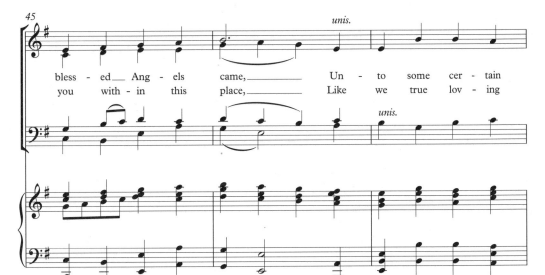

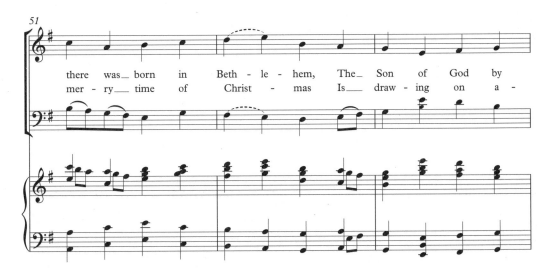

Anthem for the dedication of a church or other festivals

O how amiable

Text from Psalms 84 and 90
and Isaac Watts (1674–1748)

RALPH VAUGHAN WILLIAMS (1872–1958)
arranged by John Leavitt

Duration: *c.*4 mins

King____ and my God.
Bless - ed are they that

Bless - ed are they that

dwell in thy__ house:_____
They will be al - way__ prais - ing

dwell in thy__ house:_____

thee.

Poco più mosso ♩ = 100

Poco più mosso ♩ = 100

f sostenuto

The glo - rious Ma-jes-ty of __ the __

Lord our God be up - on us: pros - per

thou the __ work of our hands up - on ____ us.

O   pros - per thou_____ our   han - dy-work,_____

___   O   pros - per thou our_ han - dy - work._____

ff

O God, our help in a - ges past, Our

hope for years to come, Our shel - ter from the

storm - y blast, And our e - ter - nal home.

He that is down need fear no fall
(The woodcutter's song)

John Bunyan (1628–88)

RALPH VAUGHAN WILLIAMS (1872–1958)
arranged by John Leavitt

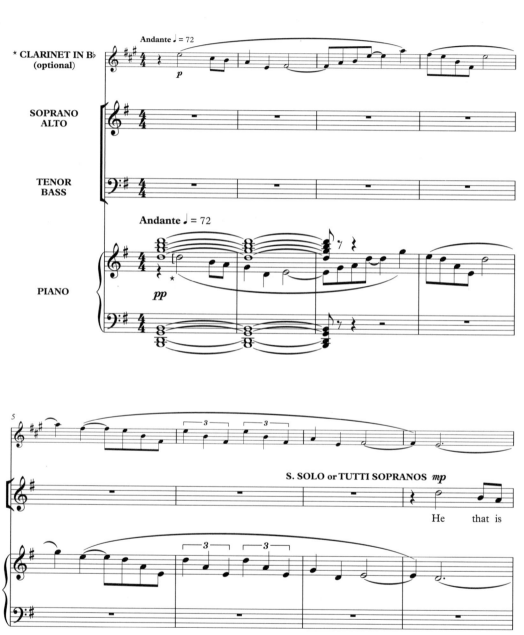

Duration: *c*.2.5 mins

*The passages between square brackets may be played by clarinet, flute, or recorder, in which case they should not be played on the piano.

This song was originally written for the stage-work *The Pilgrim's Progress*. It differs considerably from the present version, and is in the key of A flat.

-tent with what I have, Lit - tle be it or_ much;_____ And, Lord,_ con-

p legato

-tent - ment still I crave, Be - cause thou sav - est such._____

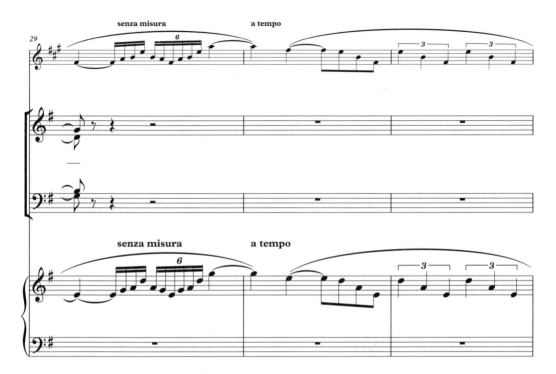

At the name of Jesus

Caroline M. Noel (1817–77)

Tune: 'KING'S WESTON'
RALPH VAUGHAN WILLIAMS (1872–1958)
arranged by John Leavitt

Duration: c.11.5 mins

Ev - 'ry tongue con - fess_____ him King of glo - ry

All the An - gel fa - ces, All the hosts of

now; 'Tis the Fa - ther's plea - sure

light, Thrones and do - mi - na - tions,

We should call him Lord, Who from the be - gin - ning Was the

Stars up - on their way, All the heav'n - ly or - ders, In their

migh - ty Word.

great ar - - ray.

3. Hum-bled for a sea - - son, To re-ceive a

dim.

name_____ From the lips of sin - - ners

Un - to whom he came,_____ Faith - ful - ly____ he____

bore_____ it____ Spot - less to____ the____ last,_____

S. Brought it back vic - to - rious When from death_____

A. Brought it back vic - to - rious_ When from death_____ he

height, Filled_____ it with the glo - - -

Filled it with the glo - ry Of that per - - fect

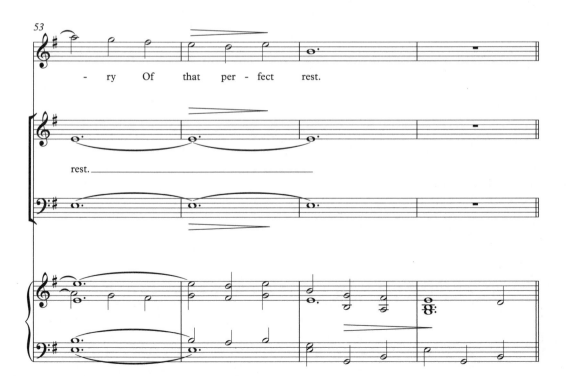

- ry Of that per - fect rest.

rest._____

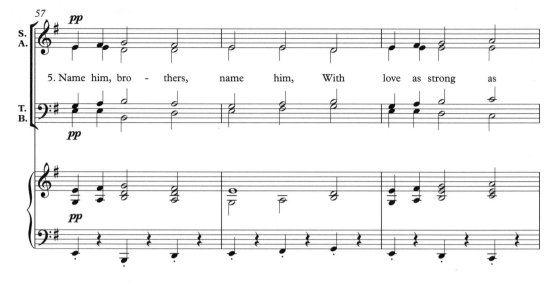

5. Name him, bro - thers, name him, With love as strong as

death,_____ But with awe and won - der,

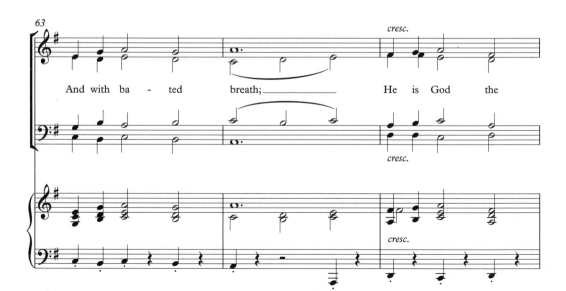

And with ba - ted breath;_____ He is God the

Sa - - viour, He is Christ the Lord,_____

dim.
Ev - er to be wor - shipped, Trust-ed and__ a -

DESCANT *mf*
6. In your hearts__ en -

DESC.

S.
A.

p   *unis. mf*
- dored._____ 6. In your hearts en - throne him;

T.
B.

unis.

76

-throne him;   There___ let him   sub - due

There let him   sub - due   All that is   not   ho - ly,

80

All   that   is___ not   ho - - - - ly,

All that is   not   true: Crown him as   your   cap - tain

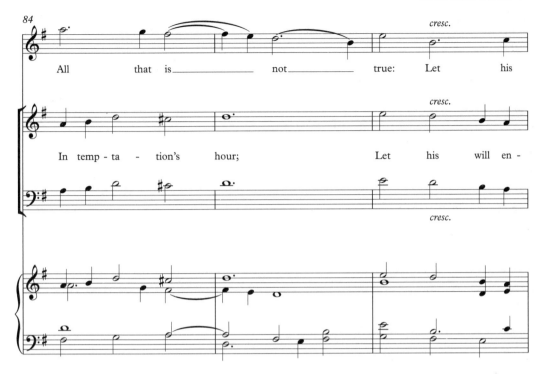

84

All that is_____ not_____ true: Let his

In temp - ta - tion's hour; Let his will en -

cresc.

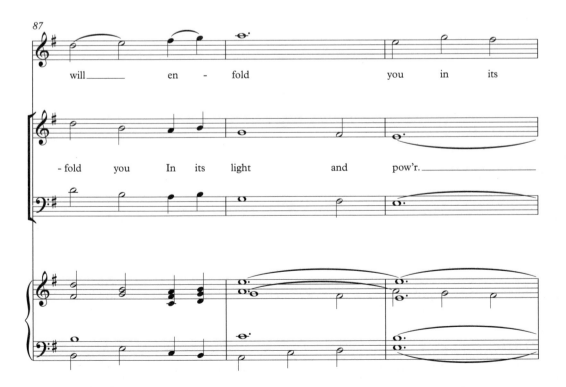

87

will_____ en - fold you in its

- fold you In its light and pow'r._____

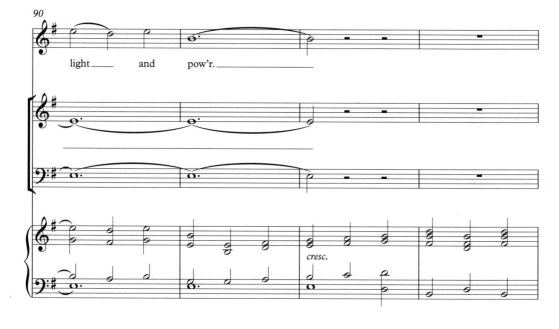

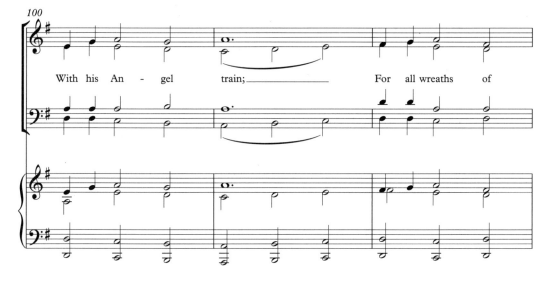

With his An - gel train;_____ For all wreaths of

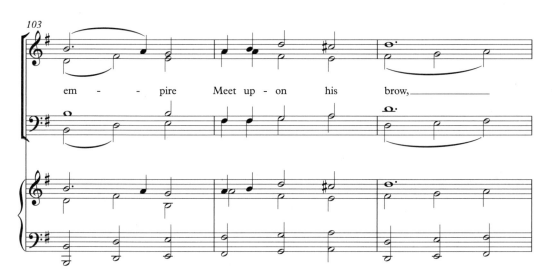

em - - pire Meet up - on his brow,_____

And our hearts con - fess him King of glo - ry now.

Let us now praise famous men

Ecclesiasticus 44

RALPH VAUGHAN WILLIAMS (1872–1958)
arranged for SATB choir by John Leavitt

Duration: *c*.2 mins

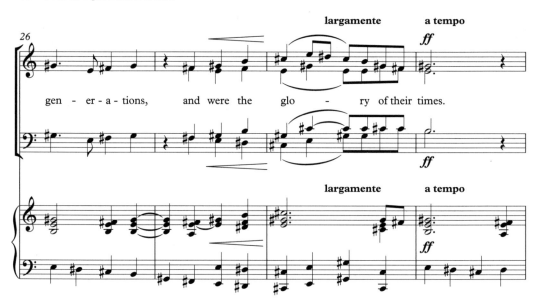

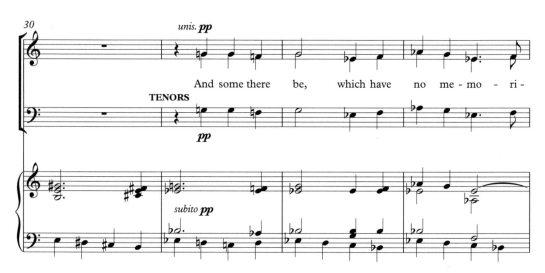

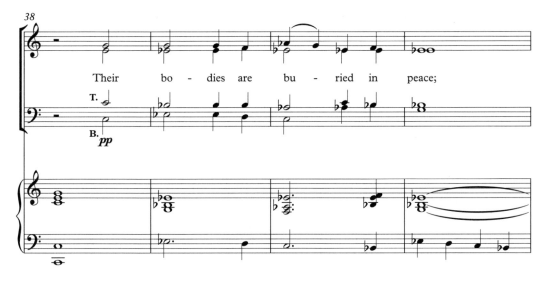

Their bo - dies are bu - ried in peace;

T.

B. *pp*

unis. cresc.

but their name liv - eth for ev - - er -

unis.

cresc.

f *cresc.*

f

cresc.

ff

- more.

ff

ff

He that is down need fear no fall
(The woodcutter's song)

RALPH VAUGHAN WILLIAMS (1872–1958)
arranged by John Leavitt